W9-ALM-046

Mysteries
OF
PREHISTORIC
—— LIFE ——

© Aladdin Books Ltd 1996

Designed and produced by
Aladdin Books Ltd
28 Percy Street
London W1P 0LD

First published in the United States in 1996 by
Copper Beech Books,
an imprint of
The Millbrook Press
2 Old New Milford Road
Brookfield,
Connecticut 06804

Editor: Katie Roden

Design:
David West Children's Book Design

Designer: Flick Killerby

Picture Research: Brooks Krikler Research

Illustrators: Francis Phillipps;
Steven Sweet and James Field – Simon Girling and Associates

Printed in Belgium

Library of Congress Cataloging-in-Publication Data
Unwin, David.
Prehistoric life / by David Unwin : illustrated by James Field... [et al.].
p. cm. -- (Mysteries of--)
Includes index.
Summary: Explores various theories of evolution and unravels the mysteries of
prehistoric time, from the first life on earth to the appearance of human beings,
using modern scientific evidence and methods.
ISBN 0-7613-0535-1 (lib. bdg.)
1. Evolution (Biology)--Juvenile literature. [1. Evolution.]
I. Field, James, 1959- ill. II. Title. III Series.
QH367.1.U58 1996
560--dc20   96-20482 CIP AC

Mysteries
OF
PREHISTORIC
LIFE

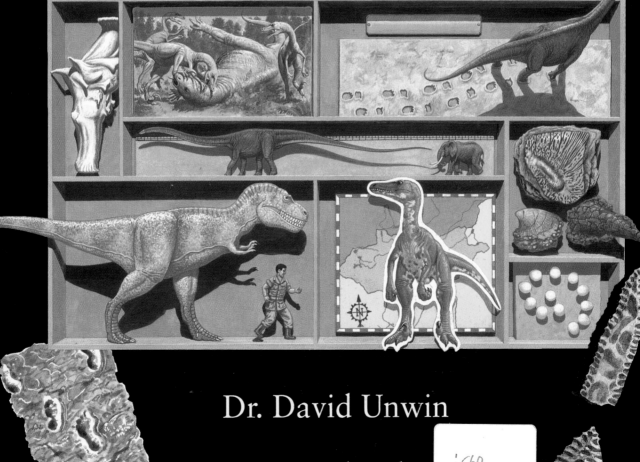

Dr. David Unwin

Copper Beech Books
Brookfield, Connecticut

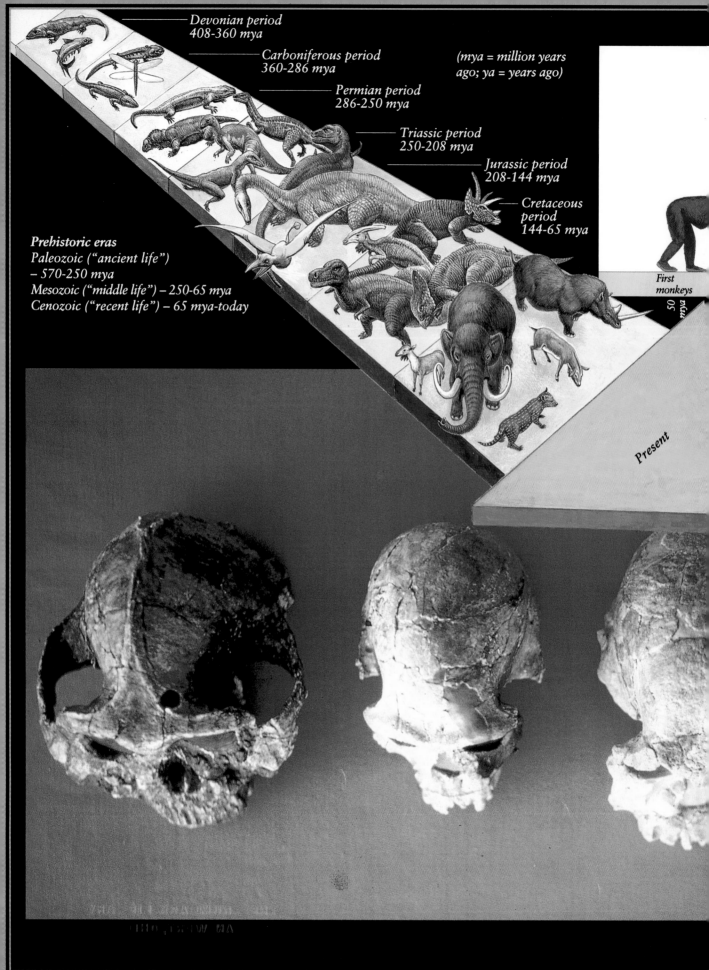

Devonian period
408-360 mya

Carboniferous period
360-286 mya

Permian period
286-250 mya

Triassic period
250-208 mya

Jurassic period
208-144 mya

Cretaceous
period
144-65 mya

(mya = million years ago; ya = years ago)

Prehistoric eras
Paleozoic ("ancient life")
– 570-250 mya
Mesozoic ("middle life") – 250-65 mya
Cenozoic ("recent life") – 65 mya-today

First
monkeys

50
mya

Present

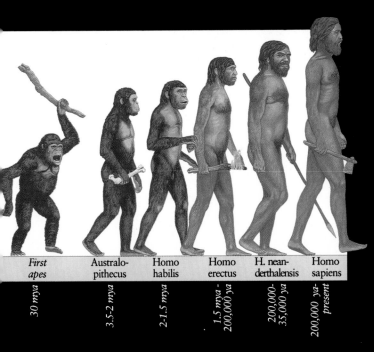

First apes	Australo-pithecus	Homo habilis	Homo erectus	H. nean-derthalensis	Homo sapiens
30 mya	3.5-2 mya	2-1.5 mya	1.5 mya - 200,000 ya	200,000-35,000 ya	200,000 ya-present

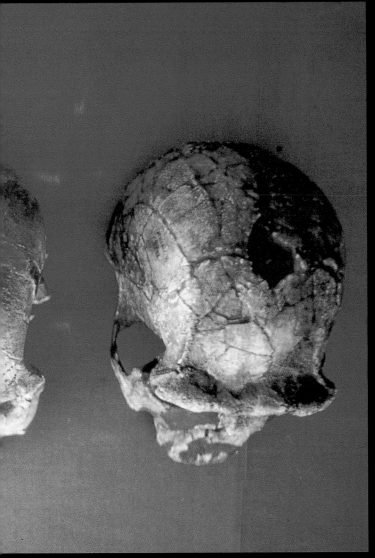

CONTENTS

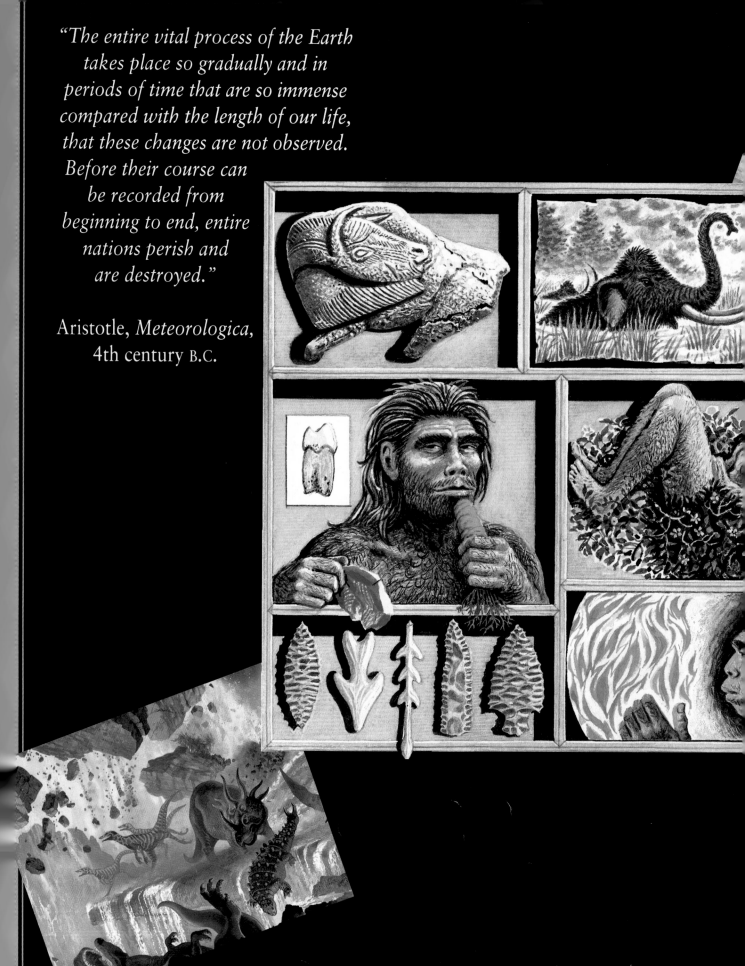

"*The entire vital process of the Earth takes place so gradually and in periods of time that are so immense compared with the length of our life, that these changes are not observed. Before their course can be recorded from beginning to end, entire nations perish and are destroyed.*"

Aristotle, *Meteorologica*, 4th century B.C.

Introduction to THE MYSTERIES

Humans have trodden the Earth for thousands of years, not knowing how old the planet is and how many past worlds lie beneath their feet. It was not until the 18th century that people realized that bones, shells, and coal found in rocks were the remains of prehistoric life – animals and plants that had lived before historical records started to be written.

Scientists then began a voyage of discovery, digging up dinosaurs, pterodactyls, mammoths, and even our ancestors. And the Earth still holds many surprises. Paleontologists (scientists who study prehistoric life) continue to find fossils that challenge their knowledge.

As information is gathered on extinct animals and plants, more branches are added to our map of the tree of life. But new discoveries also tell us how little we know. So far, we have found less than one percent of all the species that ever lived, and many puzzles remain unsolved. Why did the dinosaurs die out? How did life begin? Who were our ancestors? In deserts, under the seas, and sometimes even in our own backyards, scientists are exploring the past, solving old mysteries and finding many new ones.

"*You will observe by these remains The Creature had two sets of brains – One in his head (the usual place), The other in his spinal base.*"

B.L. Taylor, *Chicago Tribune*, on the discovery of *Stegasaurus*, 1912

What is a DINOSAUR?

Dinosaurs were an extraordinary group of animals that lived from 230 to 64 million years ago. They had upright limbs, stood erect, and swung their legs backward and forward, unlike reptiles or amphibians whose legs sprawl out to the side. There were some small dinosaurs, but most were large and some reached gigantic sizes, weighing 100 tons or more.

Dinosaurs were a diverse group of animals. Among the plant-eaters were nimble bipeds, armored ankylosaurs, and huge, plant-eating sauropods. These were hunted by meat-eating theropods, such as the dromaeosaurs and the fearsome *Tyrannosaurus*.

The dinosaur world was shared by many other groups. Ichthyosaurs and plesiosaurs – huge marine reptiles – dominated the seas, while winged pterosaurs flew through the skies. These and countless other animals and plants died out at the end of the Dinosaur Age, but some groups, such as birds and mammals, survived.

The First L I F E

According to James Ussher in 1650, the Earth and its life were formed on October 22nd, 4004 B.C. We now know that the Earth is 4.5 billion years old and that life began over 3 billion years ago.

The first life was simple. More complex life forms appeared 600 million years ago. The vertebrates began life in the seas as jawless fish. Plants invaded land first. Insects and amphibians followed, 400 million years ago. Reptiles evolved into dinosaurs and small, hairy creatures – the mammals.

THE GREENING OF THE EARTH
Plants were the very first organisms to colonize the land. Small, fernlike plants provided food and shelter for the earliest land animals, which included scorpions, spiders, insects, and even snails.

ANIMALS OR MATTRESSES?
The earliest life forms were tiny, single-celled creatures. Some formed matlike groups called stromatolites ("stone mattresses"). They still exist today in Florida and Western Australia.

PREHISTORIC PAPERWEIGHTS
Ammonites, often used as ornaments, are fossilized Mesozoic shelled squid.

What is a vertebrate?
A vertebrate is any creature with a spinal column (backbone) and cranium (skull). The first vertebrates ashore were the amphibians, 400 million years ago. They used their fins as limbs and had eight toes (later reduced to 5). Creatures without a spinal column are known as invertebrates.

RAMPANT REPTILES
As they spread into many new habitats, the early land-living reptiles underwent a surge of development. Some, such as Mesosaurus (right), went back to the water; some adopted a hot-blooded lifestyle, evolved hair, and became mammals; others took to the air; one group became the ruling reptiles – the dinosaurs.

Jawless fish
The first vertebrates were small fish such as Astraspis (above). Instead of jaws, they had a simple mouth opening and sucked up their food, which consisted of waste matter such as dead creatures and plants from the ocean floor.

Birth and death of a species
The naturalist Charles Darwin (1809-1882) developed the theory of evolution. It states that species are constantly developing to cope with changes in food supply and climate; if not, they die out.

Triassic take-off
Reptiles first flew more than 200 million years ago. Sharovipteryx (left) used a membranous wing, supported by its legs, to swoop and glide as it hunted insects in the forests of the Late Triassic period.

An "eggcellent" idea
The reptilian egg was a safe, nutritious place for the embryo (unborn baby) to grow. It allowed reptiles to roam freely and spread their species over large areas, unlike amphibians, which had to lay their eggs in water.

Coelophysis (230 mya)

Triassic murder mystery
Early reptiles dominated the land until about 250 million years ago. Then many suddenly died out, for reasons that are still unknown.

Twenty million years later, their former habitats were filled by the first dinosaurs, such as the small, meat-eating Coelophysis (left). Had the dinosaurs just taken over after a great disaster? Or did they outcompete the early reptiles?

Tiny mysteries
500 million years ago, many new life forms were appearing. Hallucigenia was one of the oddest. A caterpillarlike creature with 14 legs and spines on its back (above), no one really knows what it was.

11

The Early
MYSTERIES

Bones of dinosaurs and other large animals were first described by scientists in the 1600s, but even the Romans had dug up such remains. These probably inspired legends. Elephant skulls, which have an opening in the middle of the head, almost certainly inspired the one-eyed Cyclops featured in the ancient Greek poem *The Odyssey*, and for centuries, people believed that large fossils were the remains of animals drowned in the biblical flood.

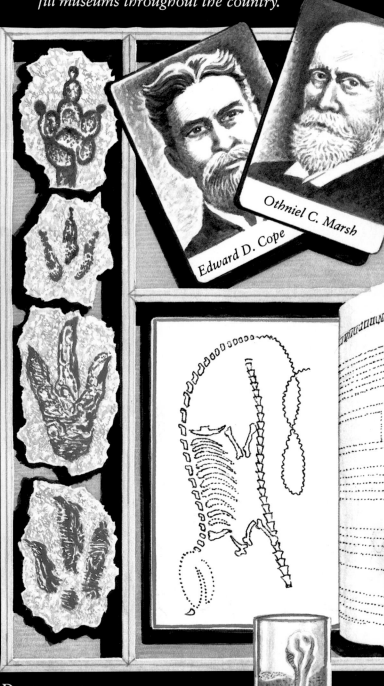

Edward D. Cope

Othniel C. Marsh

GIANT PRINTS
In 1835, Edward Hitchcock described some giant footprints found in Massachusetts. Some people believed they had been left by Noah's raven, but Hitchcock said they had come from huge birds. Only after his death were they recognized as dinosaur tracks.

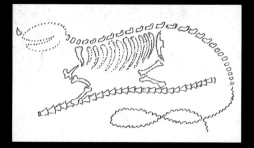

"MANTELL" PIECE *Gideon Mantell, an English doctor, was one of the first people to identify dinosaur bones. He realized they belonged to giant reptiles. He reconstructed a dinosaur (above) and named it Iguanodon.*

DRAGON BONES
In some parts of China, dinosaur bones are still thought to be the remains of dragons and are ground up for medicinal purposes.

12

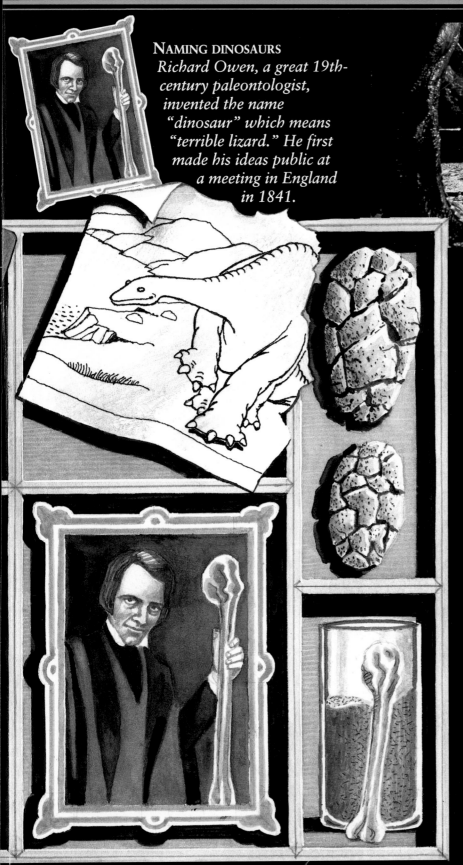

NAMING DINOSAURS
Richard Owen, a great 19th-century paleontologist, invented the name "dinosaur" which means "terrible lizard." He first made his ideas public at a meeting in England in 1841.

DINOSAURS AT THE MOVIES
Dinosaurs have appeared in many films, from King Kong *to* Jurassic Park *(above). The first dinosaur film was made in 1912 and starred a friendly sauropod called Gertie (above right).*

NESTING DINOSAURS
An expedition to Mongolia made one of the first discoveries of dinosaur eggs, in 1923. A dinosaur found with them was thought to have been an egg thief, but new findings show that it was the parent sitting on the nest (see page 36).

Dinosaurs at the Palace
The first model dinosaurs were displayed at Crystal Palace, London, in 1853. They look strange now, but they amazed everyone at the time!

Who first wrote about dinosaur bones? The first description of a dinosaur bone was published by Robert Plot in England, in 1676. He thought it was part of a giant human. The bone is now lost.

Investigations and
THEORIES

The study of dinosaurs begins with discovery and collection. Many of the best fossils come from remote parts of the world, such as the Gobi Desert of Mongolia, the Badlands of North Dakota, and even Antarctica.

Collection is a long, difficult, and delicate process. Each bone must be uncovered, dug out, and encased in plaster to prevent any damage during transportation. In the laboratory, the bones are prepared and cleaned with toothbrushes, dental picks, and tiny drills. The best-preserved skeletons are mounted for display in museums, supported by a steel frame or hung by fine wires from the ceiling. Scientists carefully measure, draw, photograph, and describe each bone.

This kind of research is the beginning of all our ideas and theories about dinosaurs. The rocks that contain fragments of dinosaurs, and other fossil animals and plants tell us much about dinosaurs and the world in which they lived.

Daily Life of a
DINOSAUR

Fossils reveal a great deal about the dinosaurs. Skeletons indicate their size and shape, while their teeth and dung show how and what they ate. The shapes of their limbs and their tracks tell us how they moved. Their skeletons may reveal the age at which they died and whether they had diseases. Blowing into models of their noses can even reproduce the sounds they made. But many mysteries remain. We do not know their body temperature or color, the number of species, or why they died out.

Prehistoric snacks
Dinosaur teeth can reveal much about their diets. Hadrosaurs had sets of teeth (right) to grind conifer needles. Bones, seeds, or leaves found in fossils also show what different dinosaurs ate.

GIANT DINOSAURS
Sauropods such as Brachiosaurus *were the largest land animals.* Seismosaurus, *found recently in North America, was up to 164 ft (50 m) long and 100 tons in weight.*

CLEVER CREATURES
Most dinosaurs had small brains (like this Tyrannosaurus *brain, right) and were as intelligent as reptiles. But some hunters had larger brains and may have been as clever as their descendants, the birds.*

PACK ATTACK
Some meat-eating dinosaurs, such as Deinonychus *(right), may have hunted in groups so they could catch large prey. Packs of* Deinonychus *were far more dangerous than a single* Tyrannosaurus.

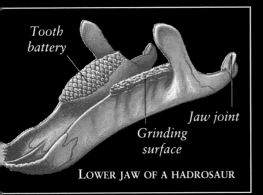

Tooth battery

Jaw joint

Grinding surface

LOWER JAW OF A HADROSAUR

ANCIENT FOOTPRINTS

There are hundreds of dinosaur tracks in ancient sand and mud flats. They show that small dinosaurs could run quickly and that many dinosaurs, even huge sauropods, moved in herds.

LAYING HABITS

All dinosaurs probably laid eggs. Most were oval-shaped and ranged from 6 inches (15 cm) wide to the size of soccer balls. Groups of eggs were usually arranged in circles, but some have been found in spiral shapes or lines. No one knows why the dinosaurs did this.

Sauropod tracks

What is a species?
A species is the basic unit of classification. The members of a species have the same characteristics and differ from all other creatures. Similar species are grouped together in a genus.

OUTWITTING THE ENEMY

Plant-eating dinosaurs had to protect themselves from the meat-eaters. Stegosaurs (above) covered themselves with spikes and spines, while the ankylosaurs (below) had a layer of "armor" and a swinging club tail.

SCARY BUT SLUGGISH

Tyrannosaurus rex *weighed 10 tons and could only reach a speed of about 21 miles (35 km) per hour. It was too heavy to be agile; if it fell while running it could be injured or killed. A human would be able to outrun it.*

DINOSAUR NAMES

Each dinosaur name is composed of 2 words: the genus (group of species), then the species. The name tells us about the animal. Velociraptor mongoliensis (left), for example, means "speedy hunter from Mongolia."

Still to SOLVE

HOW MANY DINOSAURS?

Paleontologists have found about 1,000 species of dinosaurs – a tiny fraction of all the species that ever lived. Each species was represented by millions of individuals, so, even if only one in a million dinosaurs was fossilized, thousands must still remain to be discovered and named.

More scientists than ever before are studying dinosaurs. More dinosaurs have been found in the last twenty years than over the previous 200 years. But there is much we do not know about these amazing creatures. No living animals are anything like dinosaurs, so we can only get information from fossils. Recently, there have been some important discoveries: nesting grounds, fossilized skin, a dinosaur on its nest, and several new species. Scientists are also learning more about the animals and plants that lived with the dinosaurs.

DINOSAUR IN THE DOCK

In 1992, the FBI "arrested" "Sue" the Tyrannosaurus rex, *which was at the center of a legal battle over its ownership. Nobody knows when Sue will get out of jail!*

A VERY ODD DINOSAUR

Among the peculiar dinosaurs found in the Gobi Desert of Mongolia, segnosaurs (left) are the strangest. They have a toothless beak, long neck, deep body, huge claws, and short legs. Their origins are unknown. New fossils have been found recently, so they may not be a mystery for long.

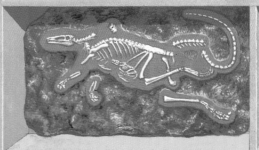

Were dinosaurs hot-blooded or cold-blooded?
At first, dinosaurs were thought to have been cold-blooded. In 1967, the idea of hot-blooded dinosaurs was proposed, based on their posture, bones, and diet. But most scientists disagree. They think dinosaurs had cold or lukewarm blood. New studies of their breathing systems suggest they are right.

DINOSAURS OF TODAY

Sir Arthur Conan Doyle's The Lost World *(right) was one of the first books to suggest that dinosaurs might still exist. Many people claim to have seen living sauropods in Africa, but no expedition has ever found them.*

CANNIBAL COELOPHYSIS

A recently discovered skeleton of Coelophysis *(see page 11) was found to contain the remains of another* Coelophysis *inside its rib cage. The animal on the inside is too large to be an unborn baby...so it is believed to have been the last meal of the larger dinosaur.*

The
LOST WORLD

Sir Arthur Conan Doyle

Brachiosaurus

The death of the dinosaurs

"Why did the dinosaurs become extinct?" is the question that paleontologists are asked most often. One dinosaur expert once counted more than 100 theories of dinosaur extinction! But it is still not known which of these, if any, is true. Perhaps there was a global catastrophe, such as a meteorite hitting the Earth (below), or perhaps it was something more simple, such as volcanic eruptions or changes in the climate. Some scientists argue that the dinosaurs did not really die out , because their descendants, the birds, still exist today.

IMPOSSIBLE SAUROPODS

Sauropods like Brachiosaurus *(right and above) ate the equivalent of 50 bales of hay every day. How did all this food manage to pass through such a tiny head?*

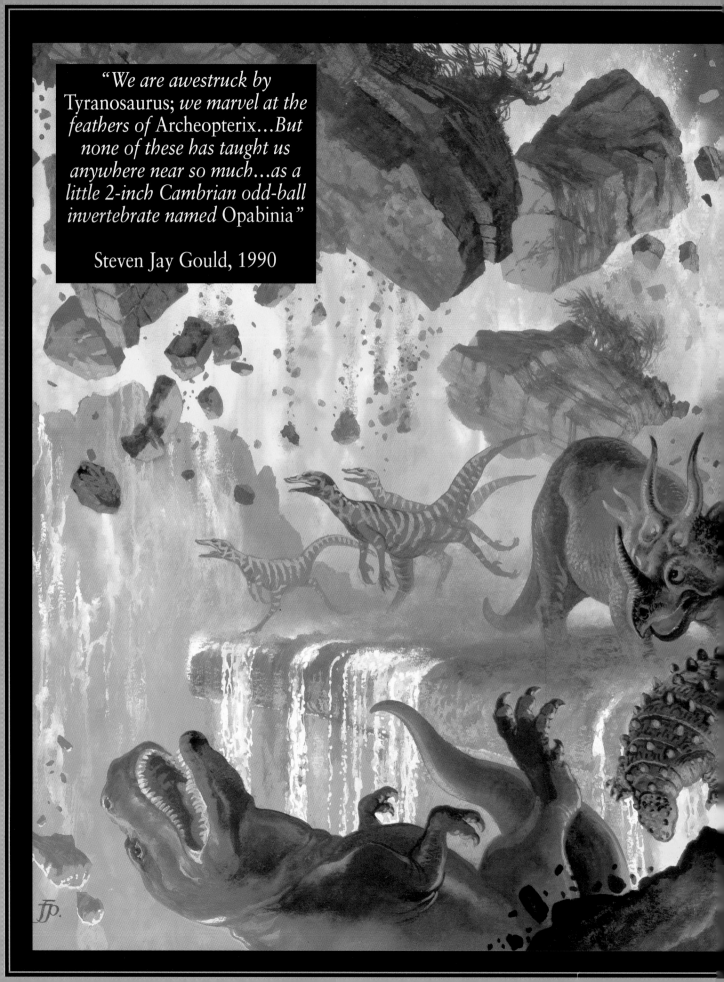

"*We are awestruck by* Tyranosaurus; *we marvel at the feathers* of Archeopterix...*But none of these has taught us anywhere near so much...as a little 2-inch Cambrian odd-ball invertebrate named* Opabinia"

Steven Jay Gould, 1990

The Diversity OF LIFE

Fossils reveal a "grand procession of life" stretching far back into the early part of the Earth's history. Large chunks of this history were dominated by particular kinds of organisms.

The Mesozoic era, for example, is often called the "Age of Dinosaurs" and the Cenozoic, which followed it, is known as the "Age of Mammals." These "Ages" did not blend smoothly into each other. Instead, they often ended with global catastrophes that swept away entire groups of animals. An event at the end of the Permian Period, 250 million years ago, killed over 95 percent of all life on Earth.

What causes these events and what actually happens while they are taking place are two of the most important questions that science has yet to answer. But these mass extinctions were not all bad. They allowed new kinds of life to appear and form new groups. Without these events, the "Age of Dinosaurs" would still be going on, and humans would not exist.

Mesozoic CHANGES

The world's last dinosaurs lived alongside many other animals and plants. Some of these organisms are still with us today, but most became extinct at the same time as the dinosaurs. The Mesozoic world was much warmer than our own and supported a rich variety of life. Instead of whales and dolphins, the seas were filled with plesiosaurs and ichthyosaurs, and the dinosaurs ruled on the land. Mammals scurried around beneath their feet while their smaller reptilian cousins – turtles, lizards, and crocodiles – lived much as they do today. The air teemed with pterosaurs and the first birds – small, feathered dinosaurs – which fluttered from treetop to treetop.

DRAGONS OF THE SKIES
Fish-eating pterosaurs flew long before birds. Most were the size of crows, but some became enormous, with 40-ft (12-m) wingspans – the size of small fighter planes.

Pterosaur ("winged reptile")

Was the atmosphere different in the Mesozoic era? Some scientists argue that the amounts of gases making up the atmosphere may have been different in the Dinosaur Age. They claim that there was more oxygen, which enabled the dinosaurs to reach giant sizes and huge pterosaurs to fly through the air. But evidence, such as tiny bubbles of prehistoric air trapped in amber, is difficult to gather and much work remains to be done.

FURRY...AND SCARED!
Mammals hid from the dinosaurs by staying small and only emerging at night. Almost all we know about them is based on their teeth, which best survived fossilization.

THE DEADLY MESOZOIC SEAS
Plesiosaurs were the fiercest marine creatures. The long-necked types ate fish, but those with short necks and vast jaws (over 6 feet (2 m) long) ate meat. Bones with bite marks show that they even ate each other.

THE MOST SUCCESSFUL CREATURES
Insects were one of the first groups to colonize the land. In good conditions, huge forms appeared, such as dragonflies with wingspans of up to 2 feet (0.5 m). Most types of insects had evolved by the Mesozoic era, so the dinosaurs must have been pestered by flies, mosquitoes, and perhaps even fleas.

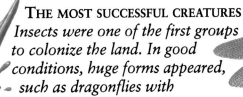

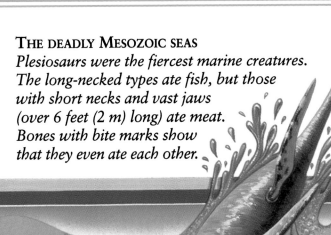

The dinosaur world
During the Mesozoic era, there were no polar ice caps and the continents were in different positions than where they are today. Previously, all the land had been joined together in one giant "supercontinent," known as Pangaea. This was now breaking into two parts – Laurasia in the north and Gondwanaland in the south. The world's climate was very mild, with warm conditions extending almost as far as the Arctic.

Laurasia

Gondwanaland

DINO FODDER
Early Mesozoic plants, upon which herbivorous (plant-eating) dinosaurs grazed, were mostly ferns, conifers, cycads, ginkgoes (left), and horsetails. Flowering plants first appeared about 100 million years ago, providing the last dinosaurs with a new diet.

Mesozoic plant and insect fossils

Early MAMMALS

A mass extinction at the end of the Mesozoic era wiped out the dinosaurs and other groups. Mammals now had a chance to flourish and many new kinds appeared. Some were very successful and their descendants – whales, tigers, bats, humans, and hedgehogs – still exist. Many species had vanished by the end of the last Ice Age, but the reason is unclear. Was it climate changes... or hungry humans?

EARLY DUMBOS
The first elephants were tuskless and pig-sized. Mammoths, mastodons, and modern elephants all descended from them.

HUNGRY HORSES
50-million-year-old horses from Germany still have remains of skin and hair, and of leaves in their stomachs.

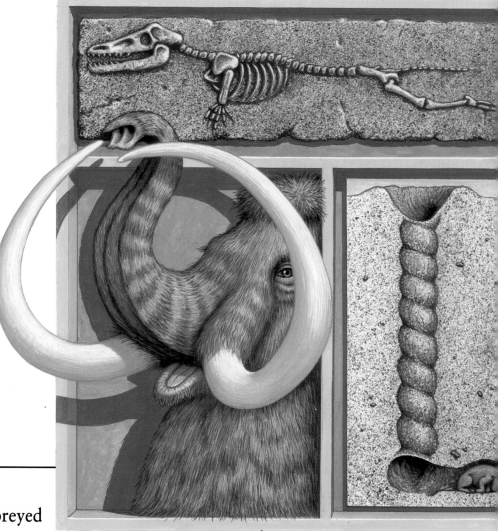

Horse-eating birds
Early mammals were preyed upon by huge, flightless birds, the phororhacids. These creatures often grew up to 10 ft (3 m) tall. With their powerful beaks, they could catch, kill, and tear apart land animals such as the first horses, which were only about the same size as modern-day sheep.

TWIST AND TURN
In 1976, mysterious, corkscrew-shaped holes were found in rocks in Nebraska (above). The fossilized remains of prehistoric beavers at the bottom of the holes gave scientists the answer – they were early burrows.

The "Giraffe-Rhinoceros"

Weighing 30 tons, and standing taller than 16 ft (5.5 m) at the shoulder, Indricotherium *was the largest land mammal of all time. It lived in Asia and probably fed on the tops of small trees.*

Living Tanks

Glyptodons *were the strangest mammals that ever lived. The ancestors of armadillos, these animals, which were up to 12 ft (3.5 m) long, had bony body armor including an armored tail.*

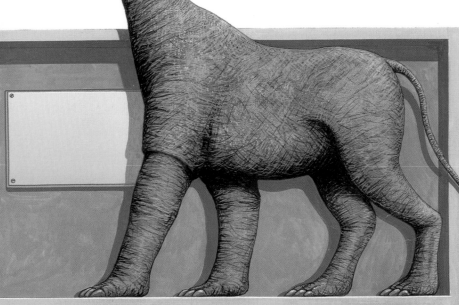

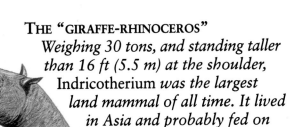

Sea Legs

The recent fossil discovery of Ambulocetus *shows that these ancestors of whales had four legs and lived on land. They returned to the water over 50 million years ago.*

What is a mammal?
Living mammals are distinguished by their hair and mammary glands (from which they get their name), but these are rarely found in fossils. Luckily, mammal teeth have a distinctive shape and are often the only parts to be preserved. Mammals also have an unusual jaw joint. Fossils clearly show the evolution of this feature over time.

Going Batty

Bats first appeared 50 million years ago. Icaronycteris, *the oldest known bat (above), was not very different from modern bats. Later fossils show that early bats could echolocate (navigate using sound waves).*

Marsupial Mystery

Marsupials (animals that rear their young in pouches) are found only in Australasia and South America. When Pangaea split, their ancestors were carried on these continents.

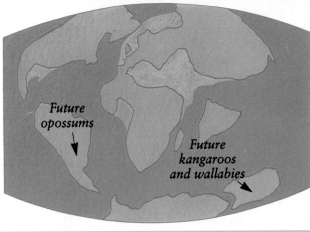

Future opossums

Future kangaroos and wallabies

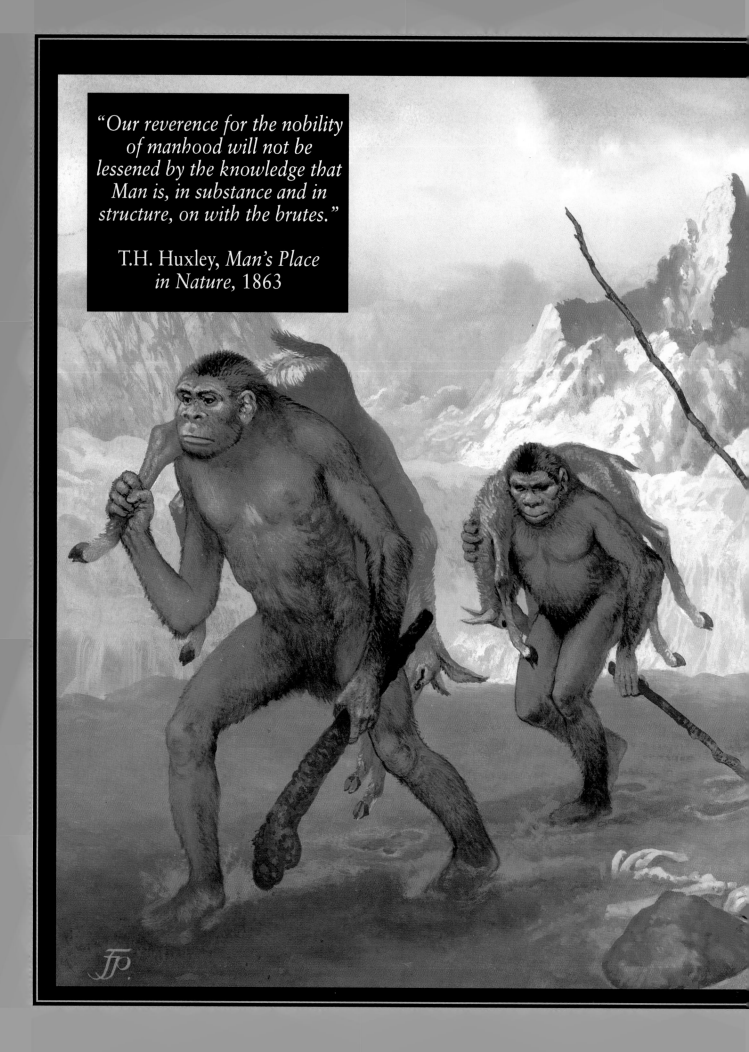

"Our reverence for the nobility of manhood will not be lessened by the knowledge that Man is, in substance and in structure, on with the brutes."

T.H. Huxley, *Man's Place in Nature*, 1863

The Emergence OF HUMANS

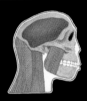

We humans are fascinated by our own ancestry. Each new discovery, even if it is only half a tooth, is greeted as a sensation. Many scientists are expending much time and a great deal of effort in the search for our ancestors, but they face a huge problem.

Our family, the hominids, has left few fossils. Most of the remains found consist of odd teeth, bones, or just fragments. Skulls are important, but they are also rare, and all the skeletons that have been found are incomplete.

With so little evidence, scientists can only guess at our origins, and arguments are common. Fortunately, major fossil findings are still being made. Work in Ethiopia has uncovered our earliest known ancestors. Over four million years old, the fossils are from a small, apelike creature which probably lived mainly in woodlands. Its teeth are similar to those of the chimpanzee and show that the human line may be more closely related to chimps than to any other living apes.

Missing Links and EARLY THEORIES

NEANDERTHAL MYTHS
Early reconstructions of Neanderthals were cartoonlike with exaggerated features (below) and stooped poses (left). New studies suggest they were much like us

Until the mid-19th century, Christians believed that humans had been created by God. Darwin (see page 11) and his supporters argued that we had descended from earlier, apelike forms and that we were simply part of the animal kingdom. This caused much anger and the "Darwinians" were ridiculed. But most people gradually accepted the idea, and the search to find our ancestors began.

At first, scientists thought that the development of humans would be a simple line of species, each of which looked a little more like us. But modern studies show that our history is complex and we have a long way to go before we unravel all the details.

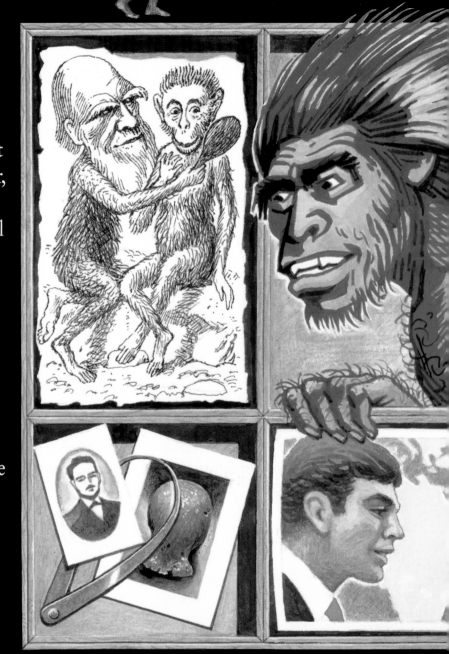

THE QUEST FOR THE "MISSING LINK"
19th-century scientists wanted to find a single "missing link" between people and apes. Dutch paleontologist Eugène Dubois thought he had found it when he discovered bones in Java in 1891. In fact, they were the remains of Homo erectus.

CONTROVERSY AND HATRED
Outrage against Darwin reached its peak in 1871, when he published The Descent of Man. *This upheld his theory that humans were part of the animal world and close to apes. Cartoons appeared ridiculing his ideas (left) and he was accused of denying Christian teachings.*

THE GIANT APES

Ten-million-year-old fossils of apes, found in Asia, were once thought to be our ancestors. Some were up to 8 feet (2.5 m) tall. In fact, they are probably related to orangutans.

TAUNG CHILD

In 1925, Raymond Dart announced the discovery of an infant man-ape in the Transvaal, South Africa. The scientific community attacked Dart, saying that he had found the remains of a chimpanzee or gorilla. But further discoveries showed that he was right. He had found evidence of our ancestor Australopithecus *(see page 30), which lived over three million years ago.*

"Taung Child"
(Australopithecus)

Out of Africa

When fossil humans were found in the 1800s, it was thought that humans originated in Asia. But early this century, Africa started to yield fossils. Finds like this skull from Kenya show that human origins must lie in Africa.

Who was "Piltdown man?"
In 1912, a strange skull was found at Piltdown, England. Was this a "missing link?" In 1952, it was shown to be a hoax – a human skull and an ape's jaw. The hoaxer's identity is still a mystery.

THE GREAT DEBATE

A new problem has divided researchers. Richard Leakey (far right) argues that the direct line leading to humans is very old; Donald Johanson (right) claims that our species split from other hominids quite recently. There is not yet enough evidence to prove either theory.

The Origin OF HUMANS

Our species, *Homo sapiens* ("wise human"), is grouped with other (extinct) species in the genus *Homo*. This and the genus *Australopithecus* make up the family *Hominidae (hominids)*. Many other genera and species have been named, but recent fossil discoveries show that few of these, if any, are real. To understand our past more fully, we must investigate the biology, habits, and history of our extinct hominid

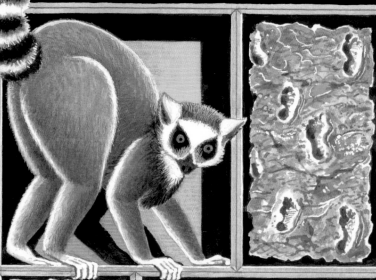

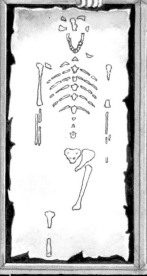

Well-traveled hominids

Our nearest relative, *Homo erectus*, was still living 200,000 years ago, alongside the first members of our own species. *Homo erectus* looked a lot like us, but had heavy eyebrow ridges, a heavy jaw, and no defined chin. Tall, narrow-hipped, and long-legged, *Homo erectus* was able to travel over long distances. The species spread from Africa to Europe, Siberia, Java, and China about a million years ago.

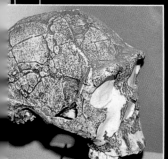

THE "SOUTHERN APE"
Three million years ago, an apelike creature, 3-4.5 ft (1-1.5 m) high, ran upright across the African plains. Australopithecus, our ancestor, had come down from the trees to eat. Large, thick teeth helped it to grind its food, which mainly consisted of fruit and leaves. But the ground was dangerous – hyenas and leopards were constantly looking for prey.

"Handy human"

Homo habilis, *from Africa, was the first to use simple tools. Fossils and tools are often found on the edges of ancient lakes and rivers – good sites to catch prey as they came to drink.*

I love Lucy

In 1975, a stunning discovery was made in Hadar, Ethiopia. Bones from a family group of at least thirteen individuals of Australopithecus *were found in sediments beside a lake. The most complete specimen, a young female, was nicknamed Lucy. She showed that* Australopithecus *had a primitive skull on top of a modern body.*

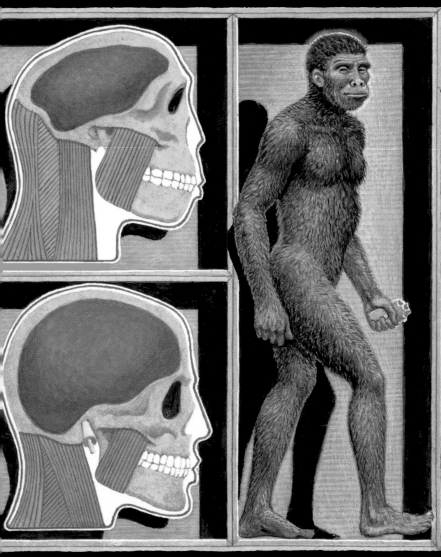

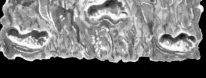

Humans stand up

Nearly four million years ago, two of our ancestors walked upright across ash deposited at Laetoli, Tanzania, by a recent volcanic eruption nearby . Their footprints were preserved in the ash and can still be seen there today. The prints show that, even at this very early stage of their evolution, humans stood upright and walked in the same way as modern humans, with long, swinging strides.

How old is our species? The earliest definite remains of Homo sapiens *are about 120,000 years old. But the Petralona skull from Greece, dated at 300-400,000 years old, is claimed by some to belong to our species, and genetic studies also suggest that we have been around for at least 200-300,000 years.*

Big Brains

Homo sapiens *(right)* has a larger (0.2642-gallons) brain than Homo erectus *(left). The first big-brained ancestor was* Homo habilis *("handy man"). Its tools suggest it was left- or right-handed, so it had "lopsided" brains like us. Skulls show that the speech areas of the brain were developed, but we will never know how it spoke.*

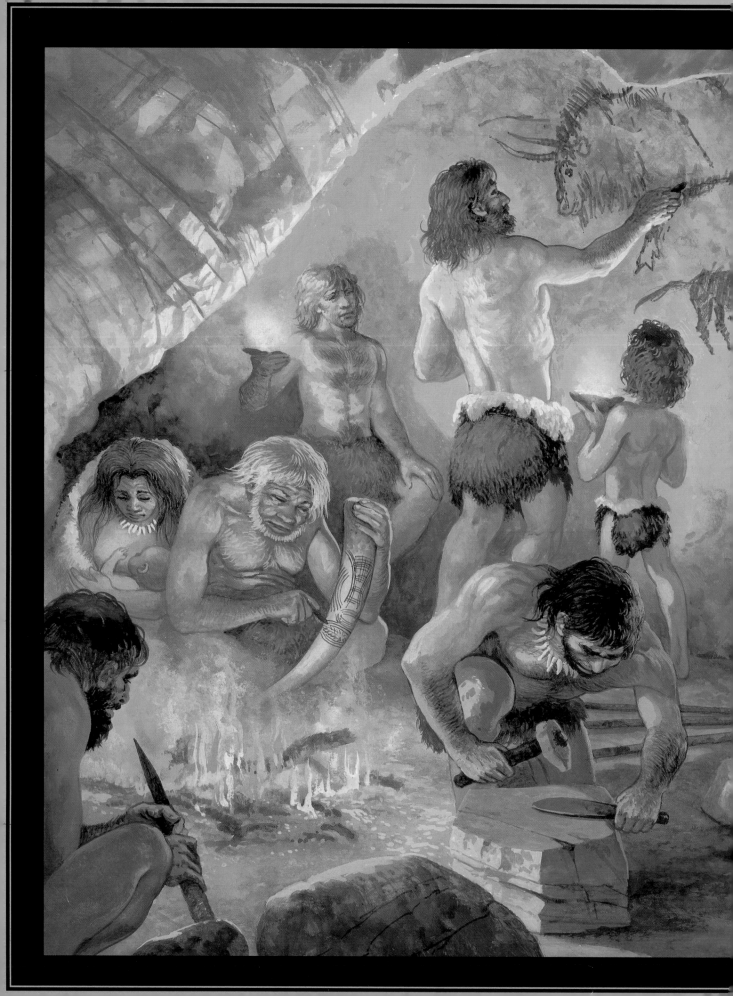

Discoveries and TECHNOLOGY

In terms of life on Earth, modern humans are the most advanced species – but not the last! We are newcomers, having only been around for a few hundreds of thousands of years.

You might think that because of this, there should be a lot of evidence for our history, but this is not the case. Speech, behavior, and social customs do not fossilize and we can only guess at them from indirect evidence like skeleton structure and tool design.

The biggest problem is the origin of our own species, *Homo sapiens*. Some scientists think that we originated in Africa about 200,000 years ago; others say that we are descended from *Homo erectus* (see page 30).

Today, genetic studies of people around the world are providing new answers to this debate. One study suggests that modern humans are descended from a single female who lived in Africa between 150,000 and 300,000 years ago. Could this incredible claim be true?

Examining our ANCESTORS

The early history of our species saw many innovations: the development of speech and language; the evolution of complex social groups; the beginnings of thought; and the appearance of religion with systems of beliefs and ceremonies. There were also many important technological innovations: the taming of fire; the invention of new materials and methods for producing clothes; shelters; and more complex, effective tools. We do not know exactly how, when, or even why many of these innovations came about, but there are hundreds of theories – and hundreds of scientists willing to test them out.

THE ICE AGE WORLD

The Ice Age (2,000,000–11,000 years ago)
Much of *Homo sapiens'* history took place during the Ice Age. In the coldest phases, glaciers spread and the sea level fell, while in the warm periods, climates were hotter than today. Such events probably caused changes in our evolution.

A KEY TO THE PAST
Just a shin bone and a tooth tell us a lot about Boxgrove man. Patterns on the tooth show that he ate raw vegetables as well as meat...and suffered from toothaches!

What happened to the Neanderthals? About 30,000 years ago, the Neanderthals suddenly vanished. No one knows if they were wiped out naturally or by their relative *Homo sapiens*.

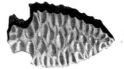
ARTY HUMANS
Art was important to the Cro-Magnons, the earliest Homo sapiens. *Their best-known works are cave paintings. Other art forms included sculptures in bone, ivory, or clay, engravings, and jewelry.*

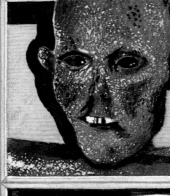
FUNERAL CUSTOMS
Neanderthals seem to have been the first to bury their dead, often with tools, bones, and flowers. Many graves contain old or diseased bodies; Neanderthals must have cared for the elderly and the sick.

TOOLS OF THE TRADE
Cro-Magnons made sophisticated tools like spearheads (above), needles, blades, and even flutes. Flint was used at first; bone, antler, and other materials came later.

THE TALKING APE
Our brain's speech areas are over two million years old. Throats able to shape words appeared one million years later, reaching today's form 300,000 years ago.

FIRE!
Humans had begun to use fire over half a million years ago. They now had protection, a source of heat, and a way of making food easier to eat.

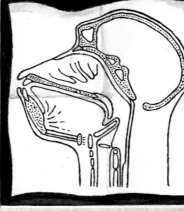
THE MYSTERIOUS ICEMAN
In 1991, the mummified body of a 5,000-year-old Neolithic man was found in a glacier. "Ötzi," complete with his tools and clothes, has solved many secrets of Neolithic life.

The Latest INVESTIGATIONS

Modern technology has enabled paleontologists to make enormous progress in the last ten years. New dating techniques, computers, scanners, X ray machines, scanning electron microscopes, and satellites have all provided new ways of searching for, collecting, and analyzing fossils. Paleontologists have also been helped by other areas of science, such as studies of genes which contain a record of the past.

How can we tell the age of fossils?
There are two ways of dating fossils: Radioactive decay, based on the fact that some elements emit radiation and change their nature over time; and fossils themselves, which are typical of certain prehistoric eras.

GENE GENIES
Scientists are now able to study our genes (the materials that give us our characteristics). Most studies have tried to discover which living ape is our closest relative; they tend to agree that it is the chimpanzee. On rare occasions, genes are preserved in fossils. If early human genetic material is ever found, it may lead to some surprising new ideas.

NESTING DINOSAURS
New discoveries are being made faster than ever, due to better excavation techniques. In 1994, an expedition to Mongolia found a dinosaur, Oviraptor, preserved sitting on a nest full of eggs (above). Previous finds had suggested that this dinosaur was a nest-raider (its name means "egg-stealer"). We now know that it was a good parent, guarding its nest even to the point of death.

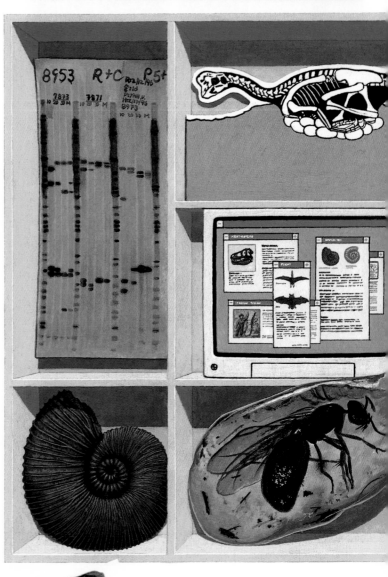

ART GALLERY FROM THE PAST
The last decade has unearthed many cave paintings. Those in Grotte Chauvet, France include the only known images of a leopard, rhinoceros, and panther. Footprints had been left by the last viewer, 30,000 years ago.

DINO DATA
Computers are rapidly becoming the scientist's most important tool. They can analyze large volumes of data and help to record the positions of findings. In the future, they will be used to produce and compare images.

FOSSIL CARE
Preparing fossils for study or display is a difficult task. Simple tools like drills, knives, and needles are used. Other equipment includes acid baths to dissolve rock around the fossil, and high-pressure air to blast off any sediment.

FACT OR FICTION?
Films and books about prehistoric life have highlighted important scientific questions. For example, could dinosaur genes be reconstructed from blood preserved in fossilized mosquitos, as suggested in Jurassic Park?

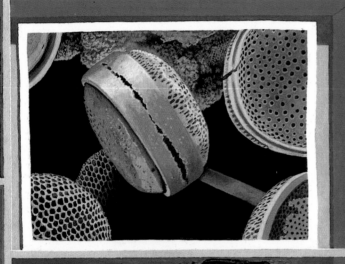

The unsolved mysteries
The science of paleontology is only a little over two hundred years old. There is so much left to discover and so many mysteries to solve that it will be hundreds or thousands of years, before scientists have even begun to exhaust all the possibilities of their research.

But paleontology does not always require expensive machines and the latest technology. Every day, amateurs all around the world collect fossils – and some of them turn out to be important pieces of the puzzle that is the "tree of life." You could go hunting for fossils tomorrow and make such a major discovery. You might even solve one of the great mysteries of the prehistoric world.

ELECTRONIC EYES
For years, paleontologists used ordinary microscopes to study fossils. Today, electronic machines allow them to see much further. The electron microscope can identify the finest structures (above). Scanners can build images of the outside and inside of skulls, providing information which would be otherwise inaccessible.

**4.6 BYA-570 MYA
PRECAMBRIAN ERA**
3.5 bya *First life appears*
640 mya *Multicelled
organisms known to exist*

570-250 MYA PALEOZOIC ERA
570-505 mya *Cambrian period*
505-438 mya *Ordovician period*
438-408 mya *Silurian period*
408-360 mya *Devonian period;
fish and amphibians appear*
360-286 mya *Carboniferous period;
amphibians dominate*
286-250 mya *Permian period;
reptiles dominate*

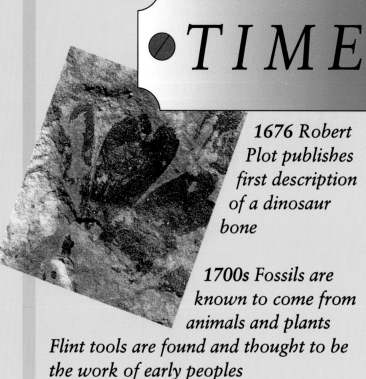

1676 Robert
Plot publishes
*first description
of a dinosaur
bone*

1700s Fossils are
known to come from
animals and plants
*Flint tools are found and thought to be
the work of early peoples*

250-65 MYA MESOZOIC ERA
250-208 mya *Triassic period; dinosaurs emerge*
208-144 mya *Jurassic period; giant dinosaurs evolve*
144-65 mya *Cretaceous period; flowers and insects appear*
65 mya *Dinosaurs are wiped out by an unknown cause*

65 MYA-PRESENT CENOZOIC ERA
50 mya *Monkeys*
30 mya *Apes*
3.5-2 mya
Australopithecus
2-1.5 mya
Homo habilis
**1.5 mya-200,000
ya** Homo erectus
**200,000-35,000
ya** Homo
neanderthalensis
200,000 ya-today
Homo sapiens

1824 Megalosaurus *is
first dinosaur to be
named scientifically*
1825 *Gideon Mantell
draws* Iguanodon
1841 *Richard Owen
names dinosaurs*
1853 *First model
dinosaurs go on display
at Crystal Palace,
London, England*

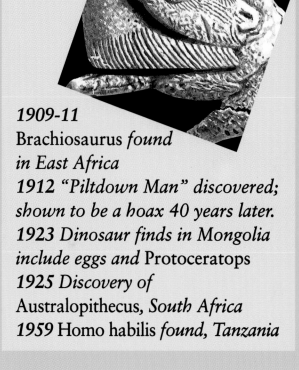

1856 Neanderthal fossil found, Germany
1858 First dinosaur skeleton,

Hadrosaurus, *discovered*
in North America
1861 Discovery of
Archaeopteryx *(the*
world's oldest bird)
1865 First discovery of
Stone Age art, France
1868 Remains of
Cro-Magnon humans
discovered, France

1909-11
Brachiosaurus *found*
in East Africa
1912 "Piltdown Man" discovered;
shown to be a hoax 40 years later.
1923 Dinosaur finds in Mongolia
include eggs and Protoceratops
1925 Discovery of
Australopithecus, *South Africa*
1959 Homo habilis found, Tanzania

1871 Darwin publishes
The Descent of Man
1878 Herd of
Iguanodon
found, Belgium
1879 Stone Age
cave paintings
found, Spain
1887 Othniel C. Marsh
describes Triceratops
1891 Eugène Dubois
discovers 'Java Man'
(Homo erectus*)*

1902 Tyrannosaurus rex
discovered, USA
1906 Neanderthal
skeleton rebuilt wrongly,
misdirecting ideas about
early humans

1963 Studies show humans and chimps shared the same
ancestor only five million years ago

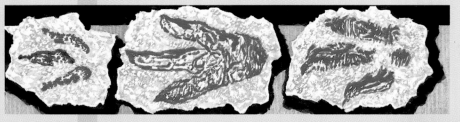

1975 "Lucy" found, Ethiopia
1983 Baryonyx found, England

1987 First discovery of
dinosaurs in Antarctica
1991 "Ötzi" found, Austria
1994 Oviraptor found nesting
1995 Argentinosaurus found
– largest dinosaur ever
1996 Finds confirm
Carcharodontosaurus saharicus *(found*
1927) as a match for Tyrannosaurus rex

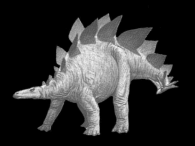

INDEX

Picture Credits (Abbreviations: t-top, m-middle, b-bottom, r-right, l-left): pages 4-5, 13t, 23br, & 30 – Frank Spencer Pictures; 8-9 – Science Photo Library; 13b – Roger Vlitos; 18, 23bm, & 37 – Bruce Coleman Collection; 29 – National Museum of Kenya / Visuals Unlimited.